ISBN 0 86112 669 6
Published by Brimax Books Ltd. Newmarket, England 1990.
Printed in Hong Kong
Produced by Mandarin Offset.

The Mouse Family
Fun
To Learn

by Rosalind Sutton
Illustrated by Pamela Storey

Brimax Books · Newmarket · England

The Mouse Family
ABC

A a

A is for Apples;
All red and good to eat,
So Archie, Daisy, Don and Flo
Fill their baskets for a treat!

8

B b

B is for Ball;
The mice are having fun,
Don throws the ball and Daisy bats,
The others have to run.

9

Cc

C is for Clock;
The mice can tell the time,
They listen as the clock strikes one,
They like to hear it chime.

D d

D is for Duck;
She dabbles in a puddle,
Don tries to count the baby ducks,
But gets into a muddle.

Ee

E is for Engine,
It goes around the track,
The mice all like to have a ride,
They go forward, they go back.

Ff

F is for Frog;
It sits upon a leaf,
It sees the mice are watching it,
And jumps off with a leap.

G g

G is for Garden;
Flo makes her garden grow,
Moss at her feet, a toadstool seat
And flowers in a row.

Hh

H is for Hat;
The mice go to the park,
They put on boots and coats and hats,
Then play until it's dark.

15

Ii

I is for Ice-cream;
The mice like this a lot,
But they all laugh as Daisy says,
"Why can't we buy it hot?"

Jj

J is for Jack-in-the-box;
Don wants to look inside,
The jack jumps out, Don gives a shout
And runs away to hide.

K k

K is for Kite;
The mice are holding tight,
For higher, higher up it goes,
It's almost out of sight.

L l

L is for Letter;
"I'll read it out," says Don.
"An invitation out to lunch!"
They put their best clothes on.

M m

M is for Magician;
He makes a magic spell,
When it goes bang the mice hide from
The smoke and nasty smell.

N n

N is for Net;
Don takes his net and line
Down to the riverbank to fish,
He hopes the day stays fine.

Oo

O is for Otter;
Flo hides behind a tree,
The otter dives and swims about,
The others come to see.

P p

P is for Penguin;
The mice go to the zoo.
Don likes the way the penguins walk,
Flo watches what they do.

23

Q q

Q is for Queen;
She wears a golden crown,
She sits upon a royal throne,
The other mice bow down.

Rr

R is for Rabbit;
He hops around the grass,
Don tries to run and catch him, but
He hops away too fast.

S s

S is for Sea;
It seems to touch the sky.
The mice sit on the sandy shore
To watch the ships go by.

Tt

T is for Toys;
The mice are in their room,
They play with teddies, tops and trains
And bang a drum, boom, boom.

U u

U is for Umbrella;
The rain falls pitter patter,
But underneath the mice are dry,
So they just sit and chatter.

Vv

V is for Violin;
Don plays a merry tune.
The other mice all like to dance
Beneath the silvery moon.

W w

W is for Wings;
The mice all try to fly.
They run and flap their tiny wings,
But cannot reach the sky.

X is for Xylophone;
An instrument to play,
The mice make merry music as
They tap and tap away.

31

Yy

Y is for Yacht;
Don sails out with his crew,
The other mice all hold on tight,
Don shows them what to do.

Z z

Z is for Zig-Zag;
The mice all love to ski,
They climb the slope, then zig-zag down
As happy as can be.

The Mouse Family

123

One little mouse is playing ball,
It bounces on the ground;
She throws it up into the air
To catch as it comes down.

2

Two little mice are on the swings,
Swinging up and down;
They swing so high that they can see
For miles and miles around.

37

Three little mice have skipping ropes,
They play a counting game;
But one little mouse trips as she jumps
And has to start again.

4

Four little mice go cycling,
They all enjoy their ride;
They pedal hard up every hill
And race down the other side.

5

Five little mice play hide and seek,
One counts behind the door;
He turns around and looks about
To find the other four.

Six little mice are on a slide,
All sliding in the sun;
They climb up to the very top
And slip down, one by one.

Seven small mice are dancing,
Together in a ring;
They raise their arms and tap their feet,
Then round and round they swing.

8

Eight mice are on a picnic,
With cookies and cakes to eat;
They sit down by the river bank
To enjoy their special treat.

49

9

Nine little mice are on the ice,
They're skating to and fro;
They like to hold each others' tails
As down the ice they go.

51

10

Ten little mice work hard at school,
They have so much to do;
They read and write all morning,
Then paint all afternoon.

The Mouse Family
Fun with Words

Washing

On Monday the mice are washing,
It is a busy day;
Some socks, some shirts and dungarees,
There is no time for play.

Reading

At bedtime Flo is reading,
Before she goes to sleep;
She tucks herself up tight in bed,
And learns her ABC.

Digging

Out digging on a Tuesday,
The mice are clearing weeds;
There is a lot of work to do
Before they plant their seeds.

Walking

Out walking in the afternoon,
The mice are holding hands;
They love to chatter as they walk
Along the golden sands.

Baking

On Wednesday the mice are baking,
Crisp cookies fill the tray;
Don and Archie help themselves,
So they are sent away.

Fishing

Fishing in the afternoon,
Is what the mice like best;
They settle by the river bank,
With fishing lines and nets.

Shopping

On Thursday the mice go shopping,
To buy some tasty cheese,
They also buy some fruit and nuts,
Some carrots and some peas.

Carrying

Now all the mice are carrying,
A very heavy load;
Each has a bag of shopping
As they walk along the road.

Eating

The mice are eating supper,
And all of them agree;
That there is nothing better,
Than golden, toasted cheese.

Cleaning

On Friday the mice are cleaning,
Each mouse has work to do;
Sweeping, dusting and polishing,
There's so much to get through.

Sliding

Sliding on a helter skelter,
Going round and round;
The mice slide from the very top,
Until they reach the ground.

Playing

That night the mice are playing,
Together they all stand;
With fiddle, drums and xylophone,
They have their own small band.

Swimming

On Saturday the mice decide,
That they would like some fun;
They all go swimming in the lake,
Then dry out in the sun.

Climbing

Now all the mice are climbing trees,
They climb up very high;
They use their tails to hold on tight,
And seem to touch the sky.

69

Swinging

Don is swinging on a rope,
He's swinging high and low;
The others come and watch him play,
They want to have a go.

Jogging

Going jogging on a Sunday,
Is what the mice like best;
But Don and Archie run too fast,
And have to stop to rest.

Sailing

The mice are sailing on the sea,
In a boat all of their own;
They float along all afternoon,
Then Archie rows them home.

Sleeping

The mice are sleeping in their beds,
It's very late at night;
And outside in the sky above,
The moon is shining bright.

The Mouse Family
Nursery Rhymes

Jack and Jill

Jack and Jill went up the hill
To fetch a pail of water;
Jack fell down and broke his crown,
And Jill came tumbling after.

Up Jack got, and home did trot,
As fast as he could caper,
He went to bed, to mend his head
With vinegar and brown paper.

Little Miss Muffet

Little Miss Muffet
Sat on a tuffet,
Eating her curds and whey;
There came a big spider,
Who sat down beside her
And frightened Miss Muffet away.

Twinkle, Twinkle, Little Star

Twinkle, twinkle, little star,
How I wonder what you are!
Up above the world so high,
Like a diamond in the sky.

Lavender's Blue

Lavender's blue, diddle, diddle,
Lavender's green;
When I am king, diddle, diddle,
You shall be queen.

Hickory, Dickory, Dock

Hickory, dickory, dock,
The mouse ran up the clock.
The clock struck one,
The mouse ran down,
Hickory, dickory, dock.

Mary, Mary, Quite Contrary

Mary, Mary, quite contrary,
How does your garden grow?
With silver bells and cockle shells,
And pretty maids all in a row.

Ring-a-ring o'Roses

Ring-a-ring o'roses,
A pocket full of posies,
A-tishoo! A-tishoo!
We all fall down.

Pat-a-Cake

Pat-a-cake, pat-a-cake, baker's man,
Bake me a cake as fast as you can;
Pat it and prick it, and mark it with B,
Put it in the oven for baby and me.

Wee Willie Winkie

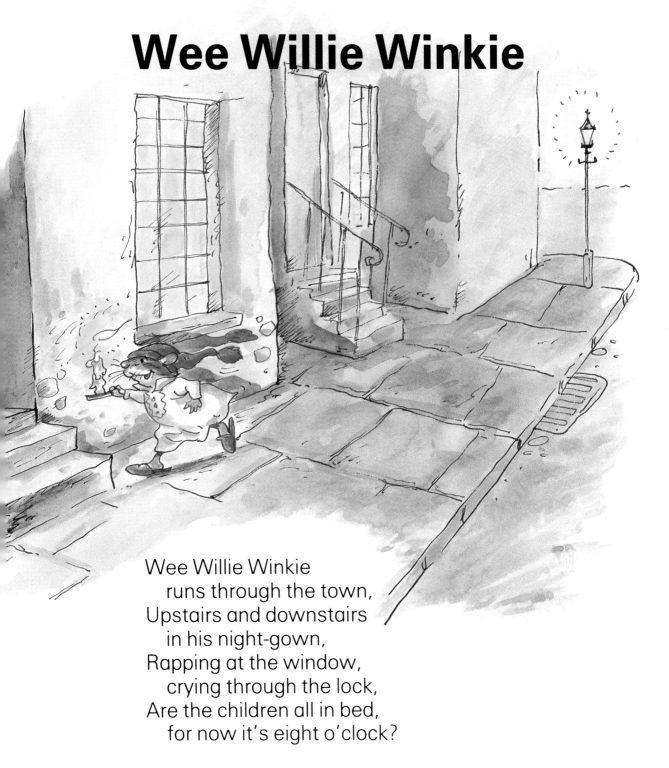

Wee Willie Winkie
  runs through the town,
Upstairs and downstairs
  in his night-gown,
Rapping at the window,
  crying through the lock,
Are the children all in bed,
  for now it's eight o'clock?

Sing a Song of Sixpence

Sing a song of sixpence,
A pocket full of rye;
Four and twenty blackbirds,
Baked in a pie.

When the pie was opened,
The birds began to sing;
Was not that a dainty dish,
To set before the king?

The king was in his counting house,
Counting out his money;
The queen was in the parlour,
Eating bread and honey.

The maid was in the garden,
Hanging out the clothes,
There came a little blackbird,
And snapped off her nose.

Rock-a-Bye, Baby

Rock-a-bye, baby, on the tree top,
When the wind blows
   the cradle will rock;
When the bough breaks
   the cradle will fall,
Down will come baby, cradle, and all.

Lucy Locket

Lucy Locket lost her pocket,
Kitty Fisher found it;
Not a penny was there in it,
Only ribbon round it.

Little Boy Blue

Little Boy Blue,
Come blow your horn,
The sheep's in the meadow,
The cow's in the corn;
But where is the boy
Who looks after the sheep?
He's under a haystack,
Fast asleep.
Will you wake him?
No, not I,
For if I do,
He's sure to cry.

The Old Woman Who Lived in a Shoe

There was an old woman
  who lived in a shoe,
She had so many children
  she didn't know what to do;
She gave them some broth
  without any bread;
She whipped them all soundly
  and put them to bed.

The Queen of Hearts

The Queen of Hearts
She made some tarts,
All on a summer's day;
The Knave of Hearts
He stole the tarts,
And took them clean away.

The King of Hearts
Called for the tarts,
And beat the knave full sore;
The Knave of Hearts
Brought back the tarts,
And vowed he'd steal no more.

Little Jack Horner

Little Jack Horner
Sat in the corner,
Eating a Christmas pie;
He put in his thumb,
And pulled out a plum,
And said, "What a good boy am I!"

Jack Be Nimble

Jack be nimble,
Jack be quick,
Jack jump over
The candle stick.

Little Tommy Tittlemouse

Little Tommy Tittlemouse
Lived in a little house;
He caught fishes
In other men's ditches.

Little Nancy Etticoat

Little Nancy Etticoat,
With a white petticoat,
And a red nose;
She has no feet or hands,
The longer she stands
The shorter she grows.

Little Betty Blue

Little Betty Blue
Lost her holiday shoe,
What can little Betty do?
Give her another
To match the other,
And then she may walk out in two.

Old King Cole

Old King Cole
Was a merry old soul,
And a merry old soul was he;
He called for his pipe,
And he called for his bowl,
And he called for his fiddlers three.

Little Tommy Tucker

Little Tommy Tucker,
Sings for his supper:
What shall we give him?
White bread and butter.
How shall he cut it
Without a knife?
How will he be married
Without a wife?

Diddle, Diddle, Dumpling, My Son John

Diddle, diddle, dumpling, my son John,
Went to bed with his trousers on;
One shoe off, and one shoe on,
Diddle, diddle, dumpling, my son John.